MW01142199

CONTENTS

Draw or affix a map, inspirational picture or memorable photo.

1

To:

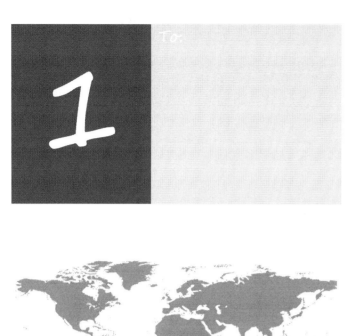

Depart.

Return.

Notes.

SUMMARY	*
Day 1	
Day 2	
Day 3	
Day 4	
Day 5	
Day 6	
Day 7	
Day 8	
Day 9	
Day 10	
Day 11	
Day 12	
Day 13	
Day 14	
Day 15	
Day 16	
Day 17	
Day 18	
Day 19	
Day 20	
Day 21	

*Use this column to sum mileage, budgets or expenditure.
Daily totals can be brought forwards from the following pages.

TRIP 1 – PLANNER

Day No.	Time	Activity (travel, check in, hire, visit, shop, eat, rest)	Distance (if applicable)	Duration	Booked	Deposit	Paid	Cost
Date	:			:				
	:			:				
	:			:				
	:			:				
	:			:				
	Total							

Accommodation   Camp o   Hostel o   B&B o   Self-cater o   Hotel o   Friends o

Day No.	Time	Activity (travel, check in, hire, visit, shop, eat, rest)	Distance (if applicable)	Duration	Booked	Deposit	Paid	Cost
Date	:			:				
	:			:				
	:			:				
	:			:				
	:			:				
	Total							

Accommodation   Camp o   Hostel o   B&B o   Self-cater o   Hotel o   Friends o

Day No.	Time	Activity (travel, check in, hire, visit, shop, eat, rest)	Distance (if applicable)	Duration	Booked	Deposit	Paid	Cost
Date	:			:				
	:			:				
	:			:				
	:			:				
	:			:				
	Total							

Accommodation   Camp o   Hostel o   B&B o   Self-cater o   Hotel o   Friends o

Day No.									

Time	Activity (travel, check in, hire, visit, shop, eat, rest)	Distance (if applicable)	Duration	Booked	Deposit	Paid	Cost
:			:				
:			:				
:			:				
:			:				
:			:				
Total							

Date

Accommodation   Camp ○ Hostel ○ B&B ○ Self-cater ○ Hotel ○ Friends ○

Day No.									

Time	Activity (travel, check in, hire, visit, shop, eat, rest)	Distance (if applicable)	Duration	Booked	Deposit	Paid	Cost
:			:				
:			:				
:			:				
:			:				
:			:				
Total							

Date

Accommodation   Camp ○ Hostel ○ B&B ○ Self-cater ○ Hotel ○ Friends ○

Day No.									

Time	Activity (travel, check in, hire, visit, shop, eat, rest)	Distance (if applicable)	Duration	Booked	Deposit	Paid	Cost
:			:				
:			:				
:			:				
:			:				
:			:				
Total							

Date
Date

Accommodation   Camp ○ Hostel ○ B&B ○ Self-cater ○ Hotel ○ Friends ○

TRIP 1 - PLANNER

Day No.

Date

Time	Activity (travel, check in, hire, visit, shop, eat, rest)	Distance (if applicable)	Duration	Booked	Deposit	Paid	Cost
:			:				
:			:				
:			:				
:			:				
:			:				
Total							

Accommodation   Camp ○   Hostel ○   B&B ○   Self-cater ○   Hotel ○   Friends ○

Day No.

Date

Time	Activity (travel, check in, hire, visit, shop, eat, rest)	Distance (if applicable)	Duration	Booked	Deposit	Paid	Cost
:			:				
:			:				
:			:				
:			:				
:			:				
Total							

Accommodation   Camp ○   Hostel ○   B&B ○   Self-cater ○   Hotel ○   Friends ○

Day No.

Date

Time	Activity (travel, check in, hire, visit, shop, eat, rest)	Distance (if applicable)	Duration	Booked	Deposit	Paid	Cost
:			:				
:			:				
:			:				
:			:				
:			:				
Total							

Accommodation   Camp ○   Hostel ○   B&B ○   Self-cater ○   Hotel ○   Friends ○

Day No.	Time	Activity (travel, check in, hire, visit, shop, eat, rest)	Distance (if applicable)	Duration	Booked	Deposit	Paid	Cost
	:			:				
	:			:				
	:			:				
	:			:				
	:			:				
	:			:				
Date	Total							

Accommodation — Camp o Hostel o B&B o Self-cater o Hotel o Friends o

Day No.	Time	Activity (travel, check in, hire, visit, shop, eat, rest)	Distance (if applicable)	Duration	Booked	Deposit	Paid	Cost
	:			:				
	:			:				
	:			:				
	:			:				
	:			:				
	:			:				
Date	Total							

Accommodation — Camp o Hostel o B&B o Self-cater o Hotel o Friends o

Day No.	Time	Activity (travel, check in, hire, visit, shop, eat, rest)	Distance (if applicable)	Duration	Booked	Deposit	Paid	Cost
	:			:				
	:			:				
	:			:				
	:			:				
	:			:				
	:			:				
Date	Total							

Accommodation — Camp o Hostel o B&B o Self-cater o Hotel o Friends o

TRIP 1 - PLANNER

Day No.	Time	Activity (travel, check in, hire, visit, shop, eat, rest)	Distance (if applicable)	Duration	Booked	Deposit	Paid	Cost
Date	Total							

Accommodation   Camp ○ Hostel ○ B&B ○ Self-cater ○ Hotel ○ Friends ○

Day No.	Time	Activity (travel, check in, hire, visit, shop, eat, rest)	Distance (if applicable)	Duration	Booked	Deposit	Paid	Cost
Date	Total							

Accommodation   Camp ○ Hostel ○ B&B ○ Self-cater ○ Hotel ○ Friends ○

Day No.	Time	Activity (travel, check in, hire, visit, shop, eat, rest)	Distance (if applicable)	Duration	Booked	Deposit	Paid	Cost
Date	Total							

Accommodation   Camp ○ Hostel ○ B&B ○ Self-cater ○ Hotel ○ Friends ○

Day No.	Time	Activity (travel, check in, hire, visit, shop, eat, rest)	Distance (if applicable)	Duration	Booked	Deposit	Paid	Cost
	:			:				
	:			:				
	:			:				
	:			:				
	Total							

Accommodation   Camp o Hostel o B&B o Self-cater o Hotel o Friends o

Day No.	Time	Activity (travel, check in, hire, visit, shop, eat, rest)	Distance (if applicable)	Duration	Booked	Deposit	Paid	Cost
	:			:				
	:			:				
	:			:				
	:			:				
	Total							

Accommodation   Camp o Hostel o B&B o Self-cater o Hotel o Friends o

Day No.	Time	Activity (travel, check in, hire, visit, shop, eat, rest)	Distance (if applicable)	Duration	Booked	Deposit	Paid	Cost
	:			:				
	:			:				
	:			:				
	:			:				
	Total							

Accommodation   Camp o Hostel o B&B o Self-cater o Hotel o Friends o

TRIP 1 - PLANNER

Day No.	Time	Activity (travel, check in, hire, visit, shop, eat, rest)	Distance (if applicable)	Duration	Booked	Deposit	Paid	Cost
Date	:			:				
	:			:				
	:			:				
	:			:				
	Total							

Accommodation   Camp ○   Hostel ○   B&B ○   Self-cater ○   Hotel ○   Friends ○

Day No.	Time	Activity (travel, check in, hire, visit, shop, eat, rest)	Distance (if applicable)	Duration	Booked	Deposit	Paid	Cost
Date	:			:				
	:			:				
	:			:				
	:			:				
	Total							

Accommodation   Camp ○   Hostel ○   B&B ○   Self-cater ○   Hotel ○   Friends ○

Day No.	Time	Activity (travel, check in, hire, visit, shop, eat, rest)	Distance (if applicable)	Duration	Booked	Deposit	Paid	Cost
Date	:			:				
	:			:				
	:			:				
	:			:				
	Total							

Accommodation   Camp ○   Hostel ○   B&B ○   Self-cater ○   Hotel ○   Friends ○

Title

Date:

Weather:

Mileage:

Who with?:

Highlight

Lessons learned / Inspirations for future trips:

✳ Rating ✳

Day 2

Title

Date:

Weather:

Mileage:

Who with?:

Highlight

✳ Rating ✳

Lessons learned / Inspirations for future trips:

Title

Day
3

Date:

Weather:

Mileage:

Who with?:

Highlight

Lessons learned / Inspirations for future trips:

※ Rating ※

TRIP 1 - DIARY

Day 4

Date:

Weather:

Mileage:

Who with?:

Highlight

Title

✳ Rating ✳

Lessons learned / Inspirations for future trips:

Title

Day
5

Date:

Weather:

Mileage:

Who with?:

Highlight

Lessons learned / Inspirations for future trips:

✷ Rating ✷

Day
6

Title

Date:

Weather:

Mileage:

Who with?:

Highlight

✳ Rating ✳

Lessons learned / Inspirations for future trips:

Title

Day
7

Date:

Weather:

Mileage:

Who with?:

Highlight

Lessons learned / Inspirations for future trips:

✳ Rating ✳

Day
8

Title

Date:

Weather:

Mileage:

Who with?:

Highlight

Lessons learned / Inspirations for future trips.

Title

Date:

Weather:

Mileage:

Who with?:

Highlight

Lessons learned / Inspirations for future trips:

✳ Rating ✳

Day
10

Title

Date:

Weather:

Mileage:

Who with?:

Highlight

✳ Rating ✳

Lessons learned / Inspirations for future trips:

Title

Day
11

Date:

Weather:

Mileage:

Who with?:

Highlight

Lessons learned / Inspirations for future trips:

✳ Rating ✳

Day
12

Title

Date:

Weather:

Mileage:

Who with?:

Highlight

Lessons learned / Inspirations for future trips.

Title

Day
13

Date:

Weather:

Mileage:

Who with?:

Highlight

Lessons learned / Inspirations for future trips:

✳ Rating ✳

Day
14

Title

Date:

Weather:

Mileage:

Who with?:

Highlight

✳ Rating ✳

Lessons learned / Inspirations for future trips:

Title

Day
15

Date:

Weather:

Mileage:

Who with?:

Highlight

Lessons learned / Inspirations for future trips:

✳ Rating ✳

Day
16

Title

Date:

Weather:

Mileage:

Who with?:

Highlight

✳ Rating ✳

Lessons learned / Inspirations for future trips.

Title

Day
17

Date:

Weather:

Mileage:

Who with?:

Highlight

Lessons learned / Inspirations for future trips:

✳ Rating ✳

Day
18

Title

Date:

Weather:

Mileage:

Who with?:

Highlight

✳ Rating ✳

Lessons learned / Inspirations for future trips:

Title

Day
19

Date:

Weather:

Mileage:

Who with?:

Highlight

Lessons learned / Inspirations for future trips:

✳ Rating ✳

Day
20

Title

Date:

Weather:

Mileage:

Who with?:

Highlight

✳ Rating ✳

Lessons learned / Inspirations for future trips.

Title

Day
21

Date:

Weather:

Mileage:

Who with?:

Highlight

Lessons learned / Inspirations for future trips:

✳ Rating ✳

Draw or affix a map, inspirational picture or memorable photo.

2

SUMMARY	*
Day 1	
Day 2	
Day 3	
Day 4	
Day 5	
Day 6	
Day 7	
Day 8	
Day 9	
Day 10	
Day 11	
Day 12	
Day 13	
Day 14	
Day 15	

Depart:

Return:

Notes:

*Use this column to sum mileage, budgets or expenditure.
Daily totals can be brought forwards from the following pages.

TRIP 2 - PLANNER

Day No.	Time	Activity (travel, check in, hire, visit, shop, eat, rest)	Distance (if applicable)	Duration	Booked	Deposit	Paid	Cost
	:			:				
Date	:			:				
	:			:				
	:			:				
	:			:				
	:			:				
	Total							

Accommodation   Camp ○   Hostel ○   B&B ○   Self-cater ○   Hotel ○   Friends ○

Day No.	Time	Activity (travel, check in, hire, visit, shop, eat, rest)	Distance (if applicable)	Duration	Booked	Deposit	Paid	Cost
	:			:				
Date	:			:				
	:			:				
	:			:				
	:			:				
	:			:				
	Total							

Accommodation   Camp ○   Hostel ○   B&B ○   Self-cater ○   Hotel ○   Friends ○

Day No.	Time	Activity (travel, check in, hire, visit, shop, eat, rest)	Distance (if applicable)	Duration	Booked	Deposit	Paid	Cost
·	:			:				
Date	:			:				
	:			:				
	:			:				
	:			:				
	:			:				
	Total							

Accommodation   Camp ○   Hostel ○   B&B ○   Self-cater ○   Hotel ○   Friends ○

Day No.	Time	Activity (travel, check in, hire, visit, shop, eat, rest)	Distance (if applicable)	Duration	Booked	Deposit	Paid	Cost
	:			:				
	:			:				
	:			:				
	:			:				
	:			:				
	Total							

Date

Accommodation Camp ○ Hostel ○ B&B ○ Self-cater ○ Hotel ○ Friends ○

Day No.	Time	Activity (travel, check in, hire, visit, shop, eat, rest)	Distance (if applicable)	Duration	Booked	Deposit	Paid	Cost
	:			:				
	:			:				
	:			:				
	:			:				
	:			:				
	Total							

Date

Accommodation Camp ○ Hostel ○ B&B ○ Self-cater ○ Hotel ○ Friends ○

Day No.	Time	Activity (travel, check in, hire, visit, shop, eat, rest)	Distance (if applicable)	Duration	Booked	Deposit	Paid	Cost
	:			:				
	:			:				
	:			:				
	:			:				
	:			:				
	Total							

Date

Accommodation Camp ○ Hostel ○ B&B ○ Self-cater ○ Hotel ○ Friends ○

Day No.	Time	Activity (travel, check in, hire, visit, shop, eat, rest)	Distance (if applicable)	Duration	Booked	Deposit	Paid	Cost
	:			:				
Date	:			:				
	:			:				
	:			:				
	:			:				
	:			:				
	Total							

Accommodation   Camp o   Hostel o   B&B o   Self-cater o   Hotel o   Friends o

Day No.	Time	Activity (travel, check in, hire, visit, shop, eat, rest)	Distance (if applicable)	Duration	Booked	Deposit	Paid	Cost
	:			:				
Date	:			:				
	:			:				
	:			:				
	:			:				
	:			:				
	Total							

Accommodation   Camp o   Hostel o   B&B o   Self-cater o   Hotel o   Friends o

Day No.	Time	Activity (travel, check in, hire, visit, shop, eat, rest)	Distance (if applicable)	Duration	Booked	Deposit	Paid	Cost
	:			:				
Date	:			:				
	:			:				
	:			:				
	:			:				
	:			:				
	Total							

Accommodation   Camp o   Hostel o   B&B o   Self-cater o   Hotel o   Friends o

Day No.	Time	Activity (travel, check in, hire, visit, shop, eat, rest)	Distance (if applicable)	Duration	Booked	Deposit	Paid	Cost
Date	:			:				
	:			:				
	:			:				
	:			:				
	:			:				
	:			:				
	Total							

Accommodation   Camp o   Hostel o   B&B o   Self-cater o   Hotel o   Friends o

Day No.	Time	Activity (travel, check in, hire, visit, shop, eat, rest)	Distance (if applicable)	Duration	Booked	Deposit	Paid	Cost
Date	:			:				
	:			:				
	:			:				
	:			:				
	:			:				
	:			:				
	Total							

Accommodation   Camp o   Hostel o   B&B o   Self-cater o   Hotel o   Friends o

Day No.	Time	Activity (travel, check in, hire, visit, shop, eat, rest)	Distance (if applicable)	Duration	Booked	Deposit	Paid	Cost
Date	:			:				
	:			:				
	:			:				
	:			:				
	:			:				
	:			:				
	Total							

Accommodation   Camp o   Hostel o   B&B o   Self-cater o   Hotel o   Friends o

TRIP 2 - PLANNER

Day No.

Date

Time	Activity (travel, check in, hire, visit, shop, eat, rest)	Distance (if applicable)	Duration	Booked	Deposit	Paid	Cost
:			:				
:			:				
:			:				
:			:				
:			:				
:			:				
Total							

Accommodation   Camp ○ Hostel ○ B&B ○ Self-cater ○ Hotel ○ Friends ○

Day No.

Date

Time	Activity (travel, check in, hire, visit, shop, eat, rest)	Distance (if applicable)	Duration	Booked	Deposit	Paid	Cost
:			:				
:			:				
:			:				
:			:				
:			:				
:			:				
Total							

Accommodation   Camp ○ Hostel ○ B&B ○ Self-cater ○ Hotel ○ Friends ○

Day No.

Date

Time	Activity (travel, check in, hire, visit, shop, eat, rest)	Distance (if applicable)	Duration	Booked	Deposit	Paid	Cost
:			:				
:			:				
:			:				
:			:				
:			:				
:			:				
Total							

Accommodation   Camp ○ Hostel ○ B&B ○ Self-cater ○ Hotel ○ Friends ○

Title

Day
1

Date:

Weather:

Mileage:

Who with?:

Highlight

Lessons learned / Inspirations for future trips:

✳ Rating ✳

😞 😐 😊

Day

2

Title

Date:

Weather:

Mileage:

Who with?:

Highlight

✳ Rating ✳

Lessons learned / Inspirations for future trips.

Title

Day
3

Date:

Weather:

Mileage:

Who with?:

Highlight

Lessons learned / Inspirations for future trips:

✳ Rating ✳

Day
4

Title

Date:

Weather:

Mileage:

Who with?:

Highlight

* Rating *

Lessons learned / Inspirations for future trips.

Title

Day
5

Date:

Weather:

Mileage:

Who with?:

Highlight

Lessons learned / Inspirations for future trips:

* Rating *

Day

6

Title

Date:

Weather:

Mileage:

Who with?:

Highlight

✳ Rating ✳

Lessons learned / Inspirations for future trips:

Title:

Date:

Weather:

Mileage:

Who with?:

Highlight

Lessons learned / Inspirations for future trips:

✳ Rating ✳

TRIP 2 - DIARY

Day
8

Title

Date:

Weather:

Mileage:

Who with?:

Highlight

Lessons learned / Inspirations for future trips.

✳ Rating ✳

Title

Day
9

Date:

Weather:

Mileage:

Who with?:

Highlight

Lessons learned / Inspirations for future trips:

✳ Rating ✳

Day 10

Title

Date:

Weather:

Mileage:

Who with?:

Highlight

Lessons learned / Inspirations for future trips.

Title

Day

11

Date:

Weather:

Mileage:

Who with?:

Highlight

Lessons learned / Inspirations for future trips.

※ Rating ※

TRIP 2 - DIARY

Day
12

Title

Date:

Weather:

Mileage:

Who with?:

Highlight

Lessons learned / Inspirations for future trips:

☀ Rating ☀

Title

Day
13

Date:

Weather:

Mileage:

Who with?:

Highlight

Lessons learned / Inspirations for future trips:

※ Rating ※

TRIP 2 - DIARY

Day 14

Title

Date: _____

Weather: _____

Mileage: _____

Who with?: _____

Highlight
_____
_____
_____

_____
_____
_____
_____
_____
_____
_____
_____
_____
_____
_____
_____
_____
_____
_____
_____
_____
_____
_____
_____
_____
_____
_____
_____

✳ Rating ✳

Lessons learned / Inspirations for future trips:

Title

Day
15

Date:

Weather:

Mileage:

Who with?:

Highlight

Lessons learned / Inspirations for future trips:

✳ Rating ✳

Draw or affix a map, inspirational picture or memorable photo.

3

To:

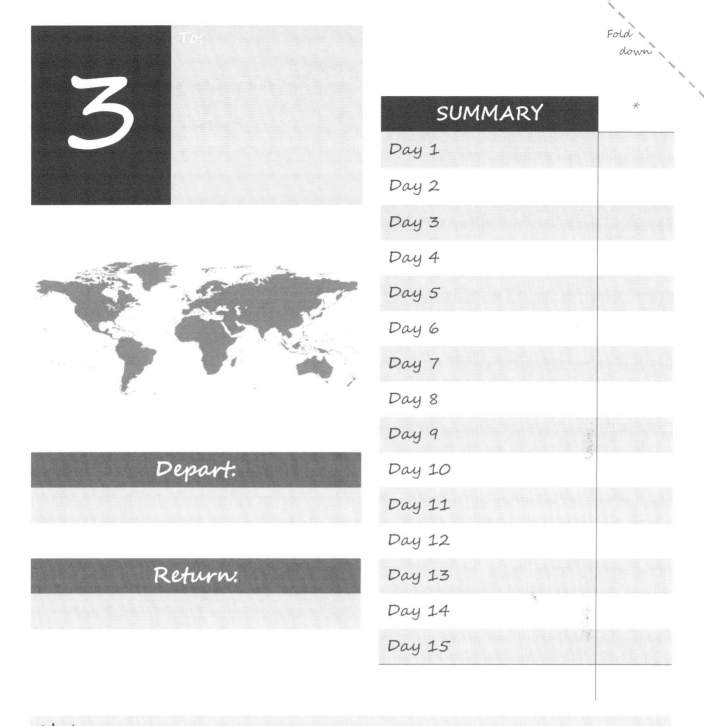

SUMMARY *

Day 1	
Day 2	
Day 3	
Day 4	
Day 5	
Day 6	
Day 7	
Day 8	
Day 9	
Day 10	
Day 11	
Day 12	
Day 13	
Day 14	
Day 15	

Depart.

Return.

Notes:

*Use this column to sum mileage, budgets or expenditure.
Daily totals can be brought forwards from the following pages.

TRIP 3 – PLANNER

Day No.	Time	Activity (travel, check in, hire, visit, shop, eat, rest)	Distance (if applicable)	Duration	Booked	Deposit	Paid	Cost
	:			:				
	:			:				
	:			:				
Date	:			:				
	:			:				
	:			:				
	Total							

Accommodation   Camp ○ Hostel ○ B&B ○ Self-cater ○ Hotel ○ Friends ○

Day No.	Time	Activity (travel, check in, hire, visit, shop, eat, rest)	Distance (if applicable)	Duration	Booked	Deposit	Paid	Cost
	:			:				
	:			:				
	:			:				
Date	:			:				
	:			:				
	:			:				
	Total							

Accommodation   Camp ○ Hostel ○ B&B ○ Self-cater ○ Hotel ○ Friends ○

Day No.	Time	Activity (travel, check in, hire, visit, shop, eat, rest)	Distance (if applicable)	Duration	Booked	Deposit	Paid	Cost
	:			:				
	:			:				
	:			:				
Date	:			:				
	:			:				
	:			:				
	Total							

Accommodation   Camp ○ Hostel ○ B&B ○ Self-cater ○ Hotel ○ Friends ○

Day No.	Time	Activity (travel, check in, hire, visit, shop, eat, rest)	Distance (if applicable)	Duration	Booked	Deposit	Paid	Cost
	:			:				
	:			:				
	:			:				
Date	:			:				
	:			:				
	:			:				
	Total							

Accommodation   Camp ○ Hostel ○ B&B ○ Self-cater ○ Hotel ○ Friends ○

Day No.	Time	Activity (travel, check in, hire, visit, shop, eat, rest)	Distance (if applicable)	Duration	Booked	Deposit	Paid	Cost
	:			:				
	:			:				
	:			:				
Date	:			:				
	:			:				
	:			:				
	Total							

Accommodation   Camp ○ Hostel ○ B&B ○ Self-cater ○ Hotel ○ Friends ○

Day No.	Time	Activity (travel, check in, hire, visit, shop, eat, rest)	Distance (if applicable)	Duration	Booked	Deposit	Paid	Cost
	:			:				
	:			:				
	:			:				
Date	:			:				
	:			:				
	:			:				
	Total							

Accommodation   Camp ○ Hostel ○ B&B ○ Self-cater ○ Hotel ○ Friends ○

Day No.	Time	Activity (travel, check in, hire, visit, shop, eat, rest)	Distance (if applicable)	Duration	Booked	Deposit	Paid	Cost
	:			:				
Date	:			:				
	:			:				
	:			:				
	:			:				
	:			:				
	Total							

Accommodation   Camp o   Hostel o   B&B o   Self-cater o   Hotel o   Friends o

Day No.	Time	Activity (travel, check in, hire, visit, shop, eat, rest)	Distance (if applicable)	Duration	Booked	Deposit	Paid	Cost
	:			:				
Date	:			:				
	:			:				
	:			:				
	:			:				
	:			:				
	Total							

Accommodation   Camp o   Hostel o   B&B o   Self-cater o   Hotel o   Friends o

Day No.	Time	Activity (travel, check in, hire, visit, shop, eat, rest)	Distance (if applicable)	Duration	Booked	Deposit	Paid	Cost
	:			:				
Date	:			:				
	:			:				
	:			:				
	:			:				
	:			:				
	Total							

Accommodation   Camp o   Hostel o   B&B o   Self-cater o   Hotel o   Friends o

Day No.	Time	Activity (travel, check in, hire, visit, shop, eat, rest)	Distance (if applicable)	Duration	Booked	Deposit	Paid	Cost
Date	:			:				
	:			:				
	:			:				
	:			:				
	:			:				
	Total							

Accommodation   Camp ○ Hostel ○ B&B ○ Self-cater ○ Hotel ○ Friends ○

Day No.	Time	Activity (travel, check in, hire, visit, shop, eat, rest)	Distance (if applicable)	Duration	Booked	Deposit	Paid	Cost
Date	:			:				
	:			:				
	:			:				
	:			:				
	:			:				
	Total							

Accommodation   Camp ○ Hostel ○ B&B ○ Self-cater ○ Hotel ○ Friends ○

Day No.	Time	Activity (travel, check in, hire, visit, shop, eat, rest)	Distance (if applicable)	Duration	Booked	Deposit	Paid	Cost
Date	:			:				
	:			:				
	:			:				
	:			:				
	:			:				
	Total							

Accommodation   Camp ○ Hostel ○ B&B ○ Self-cater ○ Hotel ○ Friends ○

TRIP 3 - PLANNER

Day No.	Time	Activity (travel, check in, hire, visit, shop, eat, rest)	Distance (if applicable)	Duration	Booked	Deposit	Paid	Cost
	:			:				
Date	:			:				
	:			:				
	:			:				
	:			:				
	:			:				
	Total							

Accommodation   Camp ○   Hostel ○   B&B ○   Self-cater ○   Hotel ○   Friends ○

Day No.	Time	Activity (travel, check in, hire, visit, shop, eat, rest)	Distance (if applicable)	Duration	Booked	Deposit	Paid	Cost
	:			:				
Date	:			:				
	:			:				
	:			:				
	:			:				
	:			:				
	Total							

Accommodation   Camp ○   Hostel ○   B&B ○   Self-cater ○   Hotel ○   Friends ○

Day No.	Time	Activity (travel, check in, hire, visit, shop, eat, rest)	Distance (if applicable)	Duration	Booked	Deposit	Paid	Cost
	:			:				
Date	:			:				
	:			:				
	:			:				
	:			:				
	:			:				
	Total							

Accommodation   Camp ○   Hostel ○   B&B ○   Self-cater ○   Hotel ○   Friends ○

Title

Day

1

Date:

Weather:

Mileage:

Who with?:

Highlight

Lessons learned / Inspirations for future trips:

✳ Rating ✳

TRIP 3 - DIARY

Day 2

Title

Date:

Weather:

Mileage:

Who with?:

Highlight

Lessons learned / Inspirations for future trips:

Title

Day
3

Date:

Weather:

Mileage:

Who with?:

Highlight

Lessons learned / Inspirations for future trips:

✳ Rating ✳

Day 4

Title

Date:

Weather:

Mileage:

Who with?:

Highlight

Lessons learned / Inspirations for future trips:

Title

Day
5

Date:

Weather:

Mileage:

Who with?:

Highlight

Lessons learned / Inspirations for future trips:

✳ Rating ✳

Day
6

Title

Date:

Weather:

Mileage:

Who with?:

Highlight

✳ Rating ✳

Lessons learned / Inspirations for future trips:

Title

Day
7

Date:

Weather:

Mileage:

Who with?:

Highlight

Lessons learned / Inspirations for future trips:

✳ Rating ✳

TRIP 3 – DIARY

Day
8

Title

Date:

Weather:

Mileage:

Who with?:

Highlight

✷ Rating ✷

Lessons learned / Inspirations for future trips.

Day
9

Title

Date:

Weather:

Mileage:

Who with?:

Highlight

Lessons learned / Inspirations for future trips:

❋ Rating ❋

Day
10

Title

Date:

Weather:

Mileage:

Who with?:

Highlight

_____
_____
_____
_____
_____
_____
_____
_____
_____
_____
_____
_____
_____
_____
_____
_____

✳ Rating ✳

Lessons learned / Inspirations for future trips:

Title

Day
11

Date:

Weather:

Mileage:

Who with?:

Highlight

Lessons learned / Inspirations for future trips:

※ Rating ※

Day
12

Title

Date:
_____
_____

Weather:
_____
_____

Mileage:
_____
_____

Who with?:
_____
_____

Highlight
_____
_____
_____
_____

✹ Rating ✹

Lessons learned / Inspirations for future trips:

Title

Day
13

Date:

Weather:

Mileage:

Who with?:

Highlight

Lessons learned / Inspirations for future trips:

✳ Rating ✳

Day
14

Title

Date:

Weather:

Mileage:

Who with?:

Highlight

※ Rating ※

Lessons learned / Inspirations for future trips:

Title

Day
15

Date:

Weather:

Mileage:

Who with?:

Highlight

Lessons learned / Inspirations for future trips:

Rating

Draw or affix a map, inspirational picture or memorable photo.

4

To:

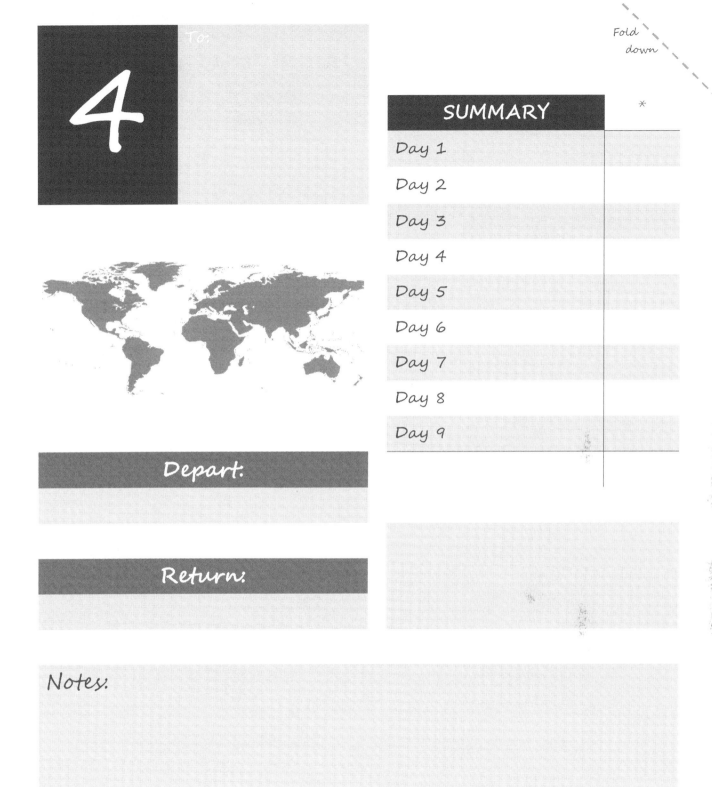

SUMMARY	*
Day 1	
Day 2	
Day 3	
Day 4	
Day 5	
Day 6	
Day 7	
Day 8	
Day 9	

Depart:

Return:

Notes:

*Use this column to sum mileage, budgets or expenditure.
Daily totals can be brought forwards from the following pages.

Day No.	Time	Activity (travel, check in, hire, visit, shop, eat, rest)	Distance (if applicable)	Duration	Booked	Deposit	Paid	Cost
	:			:				
	:			:				
Date	:			:				
	:			:				
	:			:				
	:			:				
	Total							

Accommodation   Camp ○   Hostel ○   B&B ○   Self-cater ○   Hotel ○   Friends ○

Day No.	Time	Activity (travel, check in, hire, visit, shop, eat, rest)	Distance (if applicable)	Duration	Booked	Deposit	Paid	Cost
	:			:				
	:			:				
Date	:			:				
	:			:				
	:			:				
	:			:				
	Total							

Accommodation   Camp ○   Hostel ○   B&B ○   Self-cater ○   Hotel ○   Friends ○

Day No.	Time	Activity (travel, check in, hire, visit, shop, eat, rest)	Distance (if applicable)	Duration	Booked	Deposit	Paid	Cost
	:			:				
	:			:				
Date	:			:				
	:			:				
	:			:				
	:			:				
	Total							

Accommodation   Camp ○   Hostel ○   B&B ○   Self-cater ○   Hotel ○   Friends ○

Day No.	Time	Activity (travel, check in, hire, visit, shop, eat, rest)	Distance (if applicable)	Duration	Booked	Deposit	Paid	Cost
Date	:			:				
	:			:				
	:			:				
	:			:				
	:			:				
	:			:				
	Total							

Accommodation   Camp ○ Hostel ○ B&B ○ Self-cater ○ Hotel ○ Friends ○

Day No.	Time	Activity (travel, check in, hire, visit, shop, eat, rest)	Distance (if applicable)	Duration	Booked	Deposit	Paid	Cost
Date	:			:				
	:			:				
	:			:				
	:			:				
	:			:				
	:			:				
	Total							

Accommodation   Camp ○ Hostel ○ B&B ○ Self-cater ○ Hotel ○ Friends ○

Day No.	Time	Activity (travel, check in, hire, visit, shop, eat, rest)	Distance (if applicable)	Duration	Booked	Deposit	Paid	Cost
Date	:			:				
	:			:				
	:			:				
	:			:				
	:			:				
	:			:				
	Total							

Accommodation   Camp ○ Hostel ○ B&B ○ Self-cater ○ Hotel ○ Friends ○

TRIP 4 – PLANNER

Day No.

Date

Time	Activity (travel, check in, hire, visit, shop, eat, rest)	Distance (if applicable)	Duration	Booked	Deposit	Paid	Cost
:			:				
:			:				
:			:				
:			:				
:			:				
:			:				
Total							

Accommodation   Camp ○   Hostel ○   B&B ○   Self-cater ○   Hotel ○   Friends ○

Day No.

Date

Time	Activity (travel, check in, hire, visit, shop, eat, rest)	Distance (if applicable)	Duration	Booked	Deposit	Paid	Cost
:			:				
:			:				
:			:				
:			:				
:			:				
:			:				
Total							

Accommodation   Camp ○   Hostel ○   B&B ○   Self-cater ○   Hotel ○   Friends ○

Day No.

Date

Time	Activity (travel, check in, hire, visit, shop, eat, rest)	Distance (if applicable)	Duration	Booked	Deposit	Paid	Cost
:			:				
:			:				
:			:				
:			:				
:			:				
:			:				
Total							

Accommodation   Camp ○   Hostel ○   B&B ○   Self-cater ○   Hotel ○   Friends ○

Title

Day
1

Date:

Weather:

Mileage:

Who with?:

Highlight

Lessons learned / Inspirations for future trips:

✳ Rating ✳

Day

2

Title

Date:

Weather:

Mileage:

Who with?:

Highlight

Lessons learned / Inspirations for future trips:

Title

Day
3

Date:

Weather:

Mileage:

Who with?:

Highlight

Lessons learned / Inspirations for future trips:

✳ Rating ✳

TRIP 4 - DIARY

Day 4

Title

Date:
_____
_____

Weather:
_____
_____

Mileage:
_____
_____

Who with?:
_____
_____

Highlight
_____
_____
_____

_____
_____
_____
_____
_____
_____
_____
_____
_____
_____
_____
_____
_____
_____
_____
_____
_____
_____

✳ Rating ✳

Lessons learned / Inspirations for future trips:

Title

Day
5

Date:

Weather:

Mileage:

Who with?:

Highlight

Lessons learned / Inspirations for future trips:

✳ Rating ✳

Day
6

Title

Date:

Weather:

Mileage:

Who with?:

Highlight

✳ Rating ✳

Lessons learned / Inspirations for future trips:

Title

Day
7

Date:

Weather:

Mileage:

Who with?:

Highlight

Lessons learned / Inspirations for future trips:

✳ Rating ✳

TRIP 4 - DIARY

Day 8

Title

Date:

Weather:

Mileage:

Who with?:

Highlight

✳ Rating ✳

Lessons learned / Inspirations for future trips.

Title

Day
9

Date:

Weather:

Mileage:

Who with?:

Highlight

Lessons learned / Inspirations for future trips:

✳ Rating ✳

☹ 😐 🙂

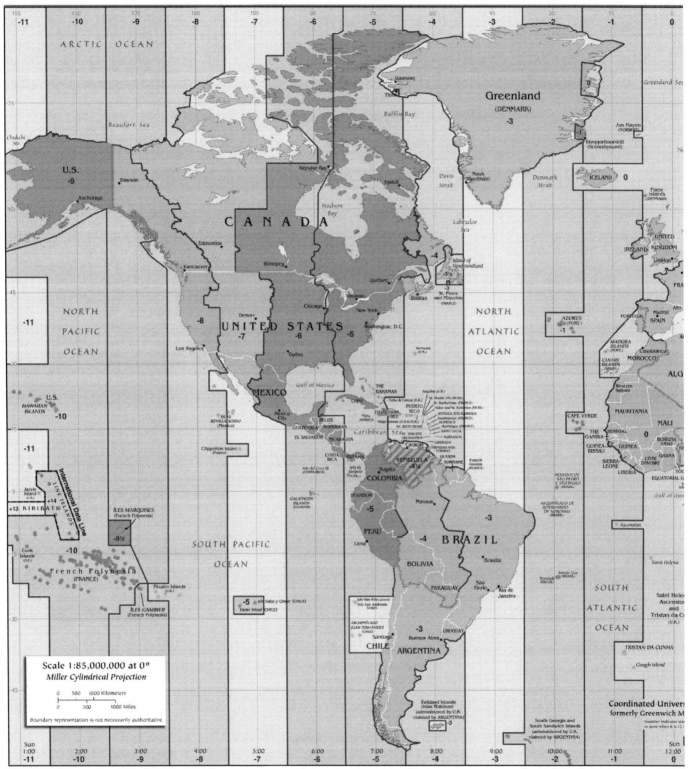

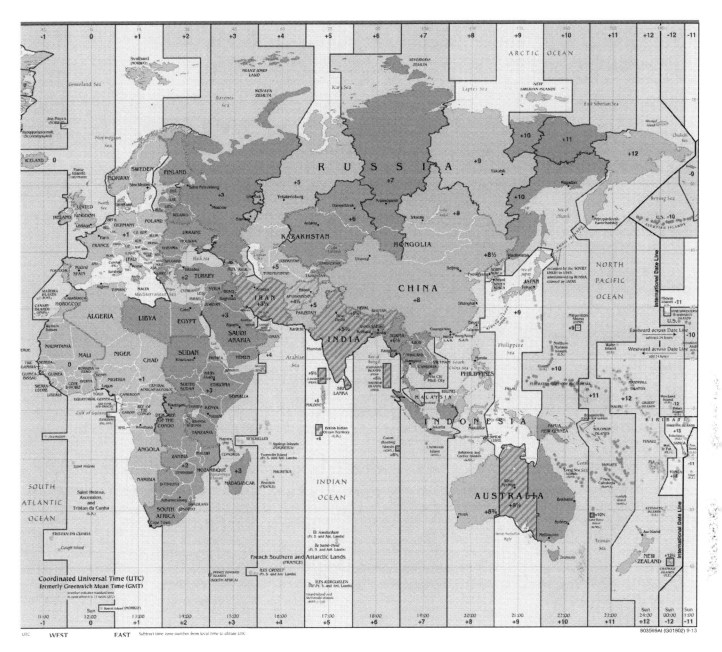

Maps kindly provided by Time Zones Boy via the Wikimedia Commons database

APPENDIX 2 – AVERAGE DAILY TOP TEMPEARTURES (°C)

North & Central America	Jan	Feb	Mar	Apr	Ma..	Jun	Jul	Aug	Sep	Oct	Nov	Dec
Albuquerque, NM	10	13	18	23	28	33	34	33	29	23	15	10
Anchorage, AK	-6	-2	0	7	15	20	19	18	13	5	-2	-7
Atlanta, GA	11	14	18	23	27	30	32	31	28	23	18	12
Belize City, Belize	26	26	28	29	30	30	30	30	30	28	27	26
Billings, MT	2	5	9	14	20	25	30	30	23	15	7	2
Boise, ID	3	7	13	17	22	27	33	32	26	18	9	3
Boston, MA	2	3	8	13	19	25	28	27	23	17	11	5
Burlington, VT	-3	-2	3	11	18	23	26	25	20	14	6	0
Calgary, AB	-1	1	4	11	16	20	23	23	18	12	3	-1
Charleston, WV	6	8	13	20	24	28	30	29	26	20	14	8
Charlotte, NC	10	13	17	22	26	30	32	31	27	22	17	12
Chicago, IL	-1	2	8	15	21	27	29	28	24	17	9	2
Columbus, OH	3	5	11	18	23	28	29	29	25	18	11	5
Dallas, TX	14	16	20	25	29	33	35	36	31	26	19	14
Denver, CO	7	8	12	16	21	27	31	30	25	18	11	6
Detroit, MI	0	1	7	14	21	26	29	27	23	17	9	2
Fargo, ND	-8	-5	2	13	21	25	28	27	22	13	3	-5
Guadalajara, Mexico	25	27	29	31	33	31	28	28	27	28	27	25
Honolulu, HI	27	27	27	28	28	28	29	29	30	29	29	28
Houston, TX	17	19	22	26	30	32	34	34	31	28	22	18
Indianapolis, IN	2	5	11	17	23	28	29	29	25	19	11	4
Jackson, MS	15	17	20	25	29	33	34	34	31	26	20	16
Jacksonville, FL	18	20	23	26	30	32	33	33	31	27	23	19
Juneau, AK	0	2	4	9	14	17	18	17	13	8	3	1
Kansas City, MO	3	6	13	19	24	29	31	31	26	19	12	5
Las Vegas, NV	14	17	21	26	32	37	40	39	34	27	19	14
Little Rock, AR	10	13	18	23	27	32	34	34	30	24	17	11

APPENDIX 2 – AVERAGE DAILY TOP TEMPERATURES (°C)

North & Central America	Jan	Feb	Mar	Apr	Ma...	Jun	Jul	Aug	Sep	Oct	Nov	Dec
Los Angeles, CA	19	20	20	22	23	25	28	28	28	25	23	20
Louisville, KY	6	9	14	20	25	30	32	31	28	21	14	8
Memphis, TN	9	12	17	23	27	32	33	33	29	24	17	11
Merida, Mexico	28	30	32	34	35	34	33	33	32	31	30	28
Miami, FL	25	26	27	28	31	32	33	33	32	30	28	26
Minneapolis, MN	-5	-2	5	14	21	26	29	27	22	14	5	-3
Milwaukee, WI	-2	0	6	14	20	26	29	27	23	16	8	1
Montreal, QC	-5	-3	3	12	20	24	27	25	20	13	6	-2
New Orleans, LA	16	18	22	26	29	32	33	33	31	27	22	18
New York City, NY	4	6	10	16	22	27	30	29	25	18	13	7
Newark, NJ	4	6	10	17	22	28	30	29	25	19	13	6
Oklahoma City, OK	9	12	16	22	26	31	34	34	29	23	16	10
Philadelphia, PA	5	7	12	18	23	28	31	30	26	19	13	7
Phoenix, AZ	20	22	25	30	35	40	41	40	38	31	24	19
Portland, OR	8	11	14	16	20	23	27	27	24	18	12	8
Salt Lake City, UT	3	6	12	16	22	28	34	33	26	18	10	3
San Francisco, CA	14	15	16	17	18	19	19	19	21	21	18	14
San Juan, Puerto Rico	28	29	29	30	31	31	31	32	32	31	30	29
Seattle, WA	8	10	12	15	18	21	24	25	21	15	11	8
Sioux Falls, SD	-3	0	6	15	21	26	29	28	23	15	6	-2
St Johns, NL	-1	-1	1	6	11	16	21	21	17	11	6	2
Toronto, ON	-2	-1	5	12	19	25	27	26	22	14	7	1
Vancouver, BC	7	8	10	13	17	20	22	22	19	14	9	6
Virginia Beach, VA	10	11	15	20	24	29	31	30	27	22	17	12
Washington, DC	7	9	14	20	25	30	32	31	27	21	15	9
Wichita, KS	6	9	14	20	25	30	34	33	28	21	13	6
Winnipeg, MB	-12	-8	-1	10	18	22	25	23	17	10	-1	-10

APPENDIX 2 AVERAGE DAILY TOP TEMPERATURES (°C)

Europe	Jan	Feb	Mar	Apr	Ma :	Jun	Jul	Aug	Sep	Oct	Nov	Dec
Amsterdam	5	5	8	11	16	18	20	21	17	13	8	6
Athens	14	14	16	19	24	29	32	32	28	23	19	15
Barcelona	13	15	16	18	21	24	28	28	26	22	17	14
Berlin	1	3	8	12	18	21	22	22	18	13	7	3
Brussels	5	5	9	12	17	19	22	22	18	14	8	6
Budapest	2	4	10	15	21	23	26	26	21	15	7	3
Copenhagen	2	2	5	9	15	18	20	20	16	11	6	3
Dublin	8	8	10	12	15	18	20	19	17	14	10	8
Edinburgh	7	7	9	12	15	17	19	19	17	13	9	7
Geneva	5	6	11	15	20	24	27	26	21	15	9	5
Innsbruck	1	4	10	15	20	23	25	24	20	14	7	2
Lisbon	15	16	18	19	21	25	28	28	26	22	18	15
London	7	8	11	14	17	21	23	23	19	15	11	8
Madrid	10	12	16	18	21	27	31	31	26	19	13	10
Marseille	10	11	14	17	21	25	28	28	25	20	14	11
Milan	6	9	13	17	21	26	29	28	24	18	11	7
Munich	2	3	8	11	17	20	22	22	18	12	6	3
Oslo	0	0	3	9	16	20	21	20	15	9	3	0
Palermo	15	15	16	18	22	25	28	29	27	23	19	16
Paris	7	8	12	16	20	23	25	25	21	16	11	8
Prague	1	2	7	12	17	20	22	22	18	12	5	2
Reykjarvik	-1	1	1	2	6	10	12	10	7	5	2	0
Rome	13	14	15	18	22	26	29	29	26	22	17	14
Seville	16	18	21	23	26	31	35	35	32	26	20	17
Stockholm	0	0	2	8	15	19	21	20	14	8	3	0
Vienna	4	6	10	16	21	24	27	27	21	15	8	5
Warsaw	0	1	6	12	18	21	22	22	17	12	5	2

APPENDIX 2 – AVERAGE DAILY TOP TEMPERATURES (°C)

Selected World Cities	Jan	Feb	Mar	Apr	Ma...	Jun	Jul	Aug	Sep	Oct	Nov	Dec
Auckland	24	24	23	20	17	15	14	15	16	18	20	22
Bangkok	31	32	33	34	33	32	32	32	31	31	31	30
Beijing	1	3	11	19	25	29	30	29	25	18	9	2
Brisbane	28	28	28	26	23	21	20	21	23	25	27	28
Buenos Aires	30	29	26	23	19	16	15	17	19	23	25	28
Cairns	31	31	30	28	27	25	25	26	27	29	30	31
Cairo	18	20	22	27	31	33	33	33	32	29	23	19
Cape Town	25	25	24	22	19	17	16	17	18	20	22	23
Delhi	21	24	30	36	40	39	35	34	34	33	28	23
Ho Chi Minh	31	32	33	33	33	31	31	31	31	30	30	30
Istanbul	7	8	10	15	20	25	27	27	24	19	13	10
Jakarta	28	29	30	31	31	31	31	31	31	31	31	30
Johannesburg	25	23	23	20	18	15	16	18	21	22	23	24
Kathmandu	15	17	21	25	26	26	26	26	25	23	20	16
Lima	26	26	26	24	22	20	19	18	19	20	22	24
Melbourne	26	26	23	20	16	13	12	13	16	18	21	24
Moscow	-6	-4	1	9	17	20	21	20	13	7	0	-3
Mumbai	31	31	33	33	33	32	30	30	30	33	34	32
Nairobi	25	26	26	24	23	22	21	22	24	25	23	23
Perth	31	31	29	25	21	18	17	18	20	22	25	28
Rio de Janeiro	33	33	32	29	28	27	26	27	28	28	29	31
Sao Paulo	27	28	27	25	23	21	21	22	22	25	25	26
Seoul	0	3	9	16	22	26	27	28	25	18	10	3
Shanghai	7	8	11	18	23	27	31	30	26	22	16	10
Singapore	29	31	31	31	31	31	30	30	30	30	30	29
Tokyo	8	9	12	17	22	24	27	30	26	20	16	11
Wellington	20	21	19	17	14	12	11	12	14	15	17	19

Several months before	Trip 1	Trip 2	Trip 3	Trip 4
Organize travel visas				
Check passport expiry dates				
Get any necessary vaccinations				
Book major travel tickets				
Book accommodation				
Plan pet care				
Monitor currency exchange rates				
Improve your language skills				
Research the culture & local attractions				
Don't specify dates on social media				
British? Need an E111 card?				
Book the time off work				

A week or two before	Trip 1	Trip 2	Trip 3	Trip 4
Check packing lists for things to buy				
Get currency if you haven't already				
Cancel any regular services or deliveries				
Check the phone tariffs abroad				
Purchase travel insurance				
Wash any clothing you want to take				

The day before	Trip 1	Trip 2	Trip 3	Trip 4
Fully charge all electronic devices...				
Now you can pack the rechargers!				
Photocopy passports				
Print tickets				
Check news, e.g. for industrial action				
Drop off keys with friends or family				
Are you contactable in an emergency?				
Check the car over & fill the fuel tank				
Check the weather forecast				
Set aside comfortable clothes to travel in				
Air travel? Check luggage regulations				

Departure day	Trip 1	Trip 2	Trip 3	Trip 4
Have any kids been to the washroom?				
Any utilities to switch off?				
Have you got tickets, cash & passports?				
Set alarms / lights on timer switches				
Lock all windows				
Do the garbage				
Close all internal doors				
Lock all external doors				

General packing list	Trip 1	Trip 2	Trip 3	Trip 4
Shoes & boots				
Socks / tights				
Underwear				
Nightwear				
Trousers / skirts				
Shorts				
Short sleeved tops				
Long sleeved tops				
Jumper/fleece				
Appropriate coats				
Suit				
Hats, scarves,				
Towels				
Swimwear				
Toiletries				
Medication				
Glasses / contacts				
Sunglasses				
Sunscreen				
Umbrella				
Sports equipment				
Writing				
Entertainment				
Guide book				
Language guide				
Jewelry / watch				

	Trip 1	Trip 2	Trip 3	Trip 4
Visas				
Passports / ID				
Drivers licence				
Tickets				
Currency / purse				
Maps				
First aid				
Insect repellent				
Tissues				
Flashlight				
Electronic devices				
Rechargers				
Socket adaptor				
Headphones				
Travel pillow				
Ear plugs				
Keys				
Laundry kit				
Plastic bags				
Gifts				
Backpack				
Packed lunch				
British? – E111				

APPENDIX 3 – PRE-TRAVEL CHECKLISTS ('TO PACK')

Build your own for specific trips e.g. winter sports, camping, beach or self-catering

	Trip 1	Trip 2	Trip 3	Trip 4

	Trip 1	Trip 2	Trip 3	Trip 4

Name:	
Address:	
E-mail:	
☎	Cell:
☎	Other:

Name:	
Address:	
E-mail:	
☎	Cell:
☎	Other:

Name:	
Address:	
E-mail:	
☎	Cell:
☎	Other:

Name:	
Address:	
E-mail:	
☎	Cell:
☎	Other:

Site:	Date:
URL:	
User/Login:	
Password or reminder:	Pin:
Notes:	

Site:	Date:
URL:	
User/Login:	
Password or reminder:	Pin:
Notes:	

Site:	Date:
URL:	
User/Login:	
Password or reminder:	Pin:
Notes:	

Site:	Date:
URL:	
User/Login:	
Password or reminder:	Pin:
Notes:	

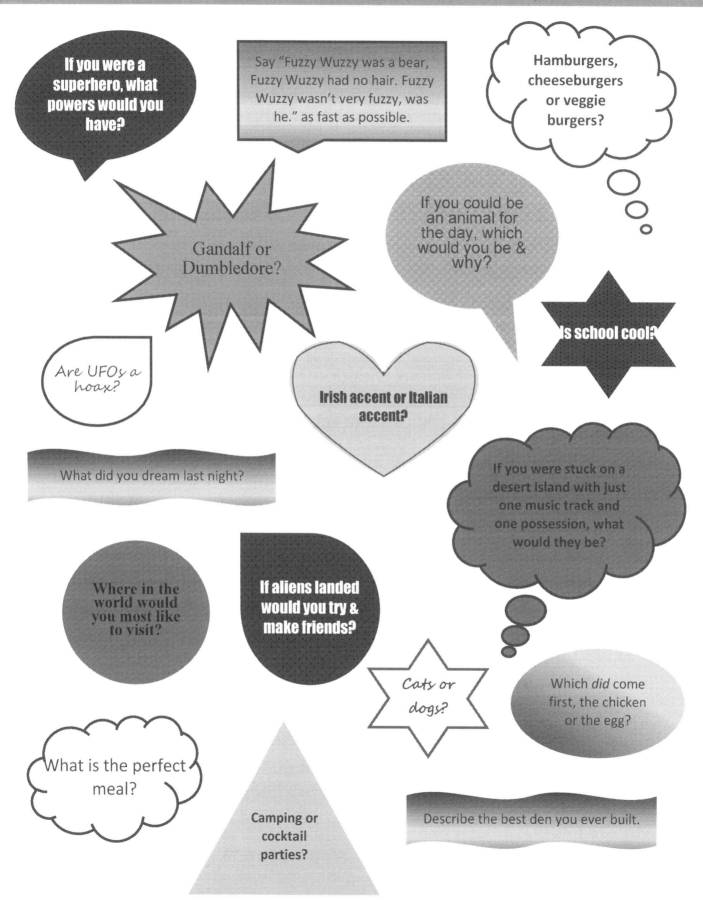

NOTES

NOTES